BHAGAT SINGH

INDIAN REVOLUTIONARY

SUSHMITA DUTTA

TRUE SIGN
PUBLISHING HOUSE

Published by True Sign Publishing House
Address: SY. No. 21/2 & 21/3, Sonnenahalli,
Krishnarajapura, Bengaluru,
Karnataka - 560049 India
E-mail: truesignbooks@gmail.com
Website: www.truesign.in

Bhagat Singh: Indian Revolutionary

Author: Sushmita Dutta

ISBN:978-93-5805-342-5

First Edition: 2023

CONTENTS

Introduction

Bhagat Singh was an Indian revolutionary who fought for India's independence against the British rule. Borrowing ideas from Bolshevism and anarchism, he electrified a growing militancy in India in the 1930s. Earlier, many leaders like Siraj-ud-daulah, Mangal Pandey, Mahatma Gandhi, Lal, Bal and Pal had sacrificed their lives in trying to deliver their motherland from the shackles of slavery.

Bhagat Singh's sense of patriotism had been embedded in him since a very young age. He yearned for an independent India free from British rule. He thought that in order to attain something as precious as independence, imperialism needed to be completely eradicated. According to him, only an armed revolution along the lines of the Bolshevik Revolution in Russia could bring about such transformation. He coined the phrase **"Inquilab Zindabad,"** which eventually became the slogan of the campaign for Indian independence.

Bhagat Singh, Shivaram Rajguru and Sukhdev Thapar were awarded capital punishment and sentenced to death in the **Lahore Conspiracy Case.** They were hanged along with their fellow revolutionaries on 23rd March 1931.

Fondly called **Shaheed Bhagat Singh**, many consider him as one of the earliest **marxists of India**. Although many of his associates were also involved in daring acts and were either hanged or died violent deaths, few came to be glorified in popular art and literature as did Bhagat Singh, who is sometimes referred to as the **Shaheed-e-Azam** or **("Great martyr.")**

Shaheed Diwas or **Martyr's Day** is celebrated to honour the commitment and courage of the freedom fighters who made the ultimate sacrifice for their motherland. Shaheed Diwas, besides being celebrated on 23rd March is also celebrated on 30th January – the day Mahatma Gandhi was assassinated.

Chapter - 1

Early Life and Childhood

Bhagat Singh was born on September 27th 1907 at a small village known as Banga in Punjab in what was then British India and is now Pakistan. His parents Kishan Singh Sandhu and Vidyavati Kaur belonged to the Sikh community. He was the second of nine children - five sons Kulbir Singh, Kultar Singh, Ranbir Singh, Rajinder Singh. Jagat Singh and three daughters Bibi Shakuntala Kaur, Bibi Amar Kaur and Bibi Prakash Kaur. Jagat Singh died very young while others lived longer, apart from Bhagat Singh's martyrdom at the age of 23 years.

During the birth of Bhagat Singh, his family members were involved in the freedom struggle and he was drawn to the **Indian Independence Movement** from a very young age. His father Kishan Singh and his uncles Ajit Singh and Swaran Singh were active in progressive politics for protesting against the 1907 **Canal Colonization Bill**. His father and uncles were also members of the Indian revolutionary organisation known as **Ghadar Party** which was led by Kartar Singh Sarabha and Lala Har Dayal. Being raised in a politically conscious household, young Bhagat Singh developed a sense of patriotism.

What was the Ghadar Party? What were its objectives?

Ghadar Party

The Ghadar Party was a revolutionary organisation with its main office in San Francisco. The majority of these revolutionaries were ex-soldiers and peasants who had moved to the USA and Canada from Punjab in pursuit of better job possibilities.

They were mostly from Jalandhar and Hoshiarpur and many of them were landless, indebted peasants. Most of them had previously served in the British Indian Army and had gained the confidence necessary to emigrate. They had travelled to these distant countries after being driven from their native country by the economic crisis and lured by the prospect of a better life.

The **Ghadar programme** was designed to plan official assassinations, disseminate anti-imperialist and revolutionary literature, coordinate with Indian troops stationed abroad, get weapons and spark a synchronised uprising across all British colonies. Lala Har Dayal, Ramchandra, Bhagwan Singh, Kartar Singh Saraba, Barkatullah and Bhai Parmanand were the driving forces behind the Ghadar Party. They wanted to incur a rebellion in India.

Features of the Ghadar Party

The Ghadar Party was a predominantly Indian-founded revolutionary group. The party included Sikh, Hindu and Muslim members. The party was primarily Punjabis.

Objectives of the Ghadar Party

The main aim of the Ghadar Party was to free India by revolutionary activities . They spread propaganda against the British and their associates through their newspaper '**Ghadar**.' The subject matter of the newspaper was related to killing of British officials, raiding government treasury, making bombs, exploding railway lines , cutting telephone lines and encouraging soldiers to revolt.

Chapter - 2

Bhagat Singh's entry into the Freedom Movement

After being sent to the village school in Banga for a few years, Bhagat Singh was enrolled in the **Dayanand Anglo-Vedic School** in Lahore which was run by Arya Samaj (a reform sect of modern Hinduism). As a child, he defied the British government by burning textbooks recommended by it.

In 1923, he joined the **National College in Lahore**, founded two years earlier by Lala Lajpat Rai in response to Mahatma Gandhi's non-cooperation movement, which urged Indian students to shun schools and colleges subsidized by the British Indian government.

At a very young age when Bhagat Singh was just 12-years-old he visited **Jallianwala Bagh** in which thousands of people were killed by the British. Bhagat Singh supported Mahatma Gandhi and the **Non-Cooperation Movement**. However, when Gandhiji called off the movement in the wake of the **Chauri Chaura** incident, Bhagat Singh was not happy at Gandhiji;s decision and hence, he joined the **Young Revolutionary Movement**.

Bhagat Singh was deeply affected by the **Jallianwala Bagh massacre (1919)** and the violence against unarmed **Akali protestors** at **Nankana Sahib (1921)**.

Chapter - 3

Anushilan Samiti

Agroup called **Anushilan Samiti** used revolutionary violence to overthrow the British rule in India during the first three decades of the 20th century. It had two branches: the **Jugantar Group** in **Kolkata** and the **Dhaka Anush ilan Samiti** in **Dhaka**. The Samiti was influenced by Bankim Chandra Chatterjee's "**Anandmath**," as well as the ideas, works and speeches of Swami Vivekanand.

Background

On March 24th 1902, Calcutta-based lawyer, **Pramathanath Mitra** founded the **Anushilan Samiti.** It was led by Barindra Kumar Ghosh, Sri Aurobindo Ghosh, Bhupendranath Datta , Deshabandhu Chittaranjan Das, Surendranath Tagore, Pulin Bihari Das, Sarala Devi, Rash Behari Bose, Jatindranath Mukherjee and Sachindranath Sanyal.

The Samiti published "**Bhavani Mandir**" (Temple of Goddess Bhavani) in 1905, which included a plan for constructing a religious sanctuary as the focal point of revolutionary operations in a remote location. In order to instill the required revolutionary mindset among Indians, Aurobindo Ghosh and Bipin Chandra Pal launched the Bengali nationalist weekly "**Jugantar**" (New Era) and its English counterpart "**Bande Mataram**" in March 1906.

Objectives

It urged its followers to recruit Indian soldiers for the revolutionary societies and obtain weapons from outside powers. They advocated military training and outlined guerrilla combat strategies and tactics in "**Vartaman Rananiti,**" which was published in 1907.

Anushilan Samiti was a well-known revolutionary organisation that operated out of Bengal in the 20th century with the goal of removing colonial authority and igniting India's independence movement. Aurobindo Ghose, Satish Chandra, Pramathanath Mitra, and Sarala Devi founded the Anushilan Samiti.

Leaders

Anushilan Samiti had leaders like Deshabandhu Chittaranjan Das, Surendranath Tagore, Jatindranath Banerjee, and Bagha Jatin. Anushilan Samiti graduate Keshav Baliram Hedgewar founded the **Rashtriya Swayamsevak Sangh (RSS).**

Anushilan Samiti Revolutionary Activities

The Samiti worked in conjunction with other revolutionary groups both in India and overseas. It was headed by the nationalists Aurobindo Ghosh and his brother Barindra Ghosh, who was influenced by ideologies such as **Italian nationalism** and Kakuzo Okakura's **Pan-Asianism**. The Samiti participated in a number of well-documented instances of revolutionary attacks against the British government and interests in India, including the first assassination attempts on British officials.

These were followed by the 1912 attempt on the Viceroy of India's life and the Seditious Conspiracy during World War I, both of which were headed, respectively, by Rashbehari Bose and Jatindranath Mukherjee.

Chapter - 4

Hindustan Republican Association (HRA) 1924

Hindustan Republican Association (HRA) was established in 1924 at village Bholachang in East Bengal by Sachindra Nath Sanyal, Narendra Mohan Sen and Pratul Ganguly as an offshoot of **Anushilan Samiti**. It was a revolutionary organisation and its main objective was to establish a **"Federated Republic of the United States of India"** through an organized and armed revolution.

Mahatma Gandhi's sudden suspension of the Non-Cooperation Movement had created a wave of dissatisfaction among the young revolutionaries. These young revolutionaries did not like the theory of non-violence. They believed that the British could be thrown out of the country by use of force and violence. At the same time, there were uprisings in other parts of the world.

The result was that a new breed of revolutionaries emerged. In the village of Bholachang in East Bengal, a meeting was held between Sachindra Nath Sanyal, Narendra Mohan Sen, Pratul Ganguly. **Hindustan Republican Association** was formed on the lines of **Irish Republican Army**. The manifesto of this revolutionary organization was "**The Revolutionary.**" The idea attracted Bhagat Singh, Chandra Shekhar Azad, Sukhdev, Ram Prasad Bismil, Roshan Singh, Ashfaqulla Khan, Rajendra Lahiri and many others who immediately joined the organization.

In 1926, Bhagat Singh founded **Naujawan Bharat Sabha** an organization that aimed to encourage revolution against British rule by rallying the peasants and workers.

He wrote and edited, Urdu and Punjabi newspapers, published in Amritsar and also contributed to low-priced pamphlets published by the Naujawan Bharat Sabha. He also wrote for **Kirti'** which was a journal published by the **Kirti Kisan Party** ("Workers and Peasants Party") and briefly for the **Veer Arjun** newspaper, published in Delhi. He often used pseudonyms, including names such as **Balwant, Ranjit** and **Vidhrohi.**

Chapter - 5

Hindustan Socialist Republican Association (HSRA)

The **Hindustan Socialist Republican Association (HSRA)** was a revolutionary party set-up by Ram Prasad Bismil and his associates to fight against British rule in India and to achieve independence for the country through an armed rebellion if necessary.

Hindustan Socialist Republican Association (HSRA), previously known as the **Hindustan Republican Army** and **Hindustan Republican Association (HRA)**, was an Indian revolutionary organisation founded by Ram Prasad Bismil, Ashfaqulla Khan, Sachindra Nath Bakshi, Sachindra Nath Sanyal and Jogesh Chandra Chatterjee.

Origins of the Hindustan Socialist Republican Association

The party was initially named **Hindustan Republican Association (HRA)** by Ram Prasad Bismil when he formed it in 1923. The main reason for the party's formation was Mahatma Gandhi's calling off the Non-Cooperation movement in 1922 because of the Chauri Chaura incident. While some of the leaders of the Indian National Congress broke away from it and formed the **Swaraja Party**, some young revolutionaries became disillusioned with the idea of non-violence and considered revolutionary movements as a way to achieve freedom.

HSRA Formation

- The constitution for the HRA was drafted by Ram Prasad Bismil in 1923 at Allahabad with the blessings of Lala Har Dayal.

- Other prominent members of the party were Sachindra Nath Sanyal and Jogesh Chandra Chatterjee (who were also a member of the Anushilan Samiti).

- The HRA formed centres at **Allahabad, Agra, Kanpur, Varanasi, Lucknow, Shahjahanpur** and **Saharanpur**.

- It also had bomb manufacturing units at **Calcutta** and **Deogarh**.

- A manifesto for the party was written by Sachindra Nath Sanyal titled 'Revolutionary'. It contained incendiary material asking the youth of the country to join the party and take part in the freedom struggle. It did not approve of the methods used by Gandhi and criticised them. The manifesto stated that it sought to achieve a 'Federal Republic of the United States of India' after overthrowing British rule.

- It also demanded universal suffrage. The material espoused a socialist society for India.

- The pamphlets were distributed in many cities in northern India.

- In 1924-1925, many young people joined the party, prominent among them being Bhagat Singh, Sukhdev and Chandrasekhar Azad.

Activities of the HSRA

- The organisation conducted many robberies and raids in an attempt to raise funds to acquire arms and ammunition.

- The most famous incident was the Kakori conspiracy. This occurred on 9th August, 1925. Members of the party looted a train carrying government money near Lucknow. An innocent passenger was killed accidentally in the process. People involved in the episode were Ram Prasad Bismil, Ashfaqulla Khan, Rajendra Lahiri and Thakur Roshan Singh. All four were eventually hanged by the government in 1927 for their involvement.

- Chandrasekhar Azad was also involved although he evaded arrest.

- In 1928, the name of the party was changed to Hindustan Republican Socialist Association (HSRA) primarily because of Bhagat Singh's insistence.

- The Simon Commission came to India in 1928. The lack of an Indian member in the commission (which was meant to deliberate on India's future government) was met with widespread condemnation and protest.

- National leader Lala Lajpat Rai was severely lathi-charged on the orders of a British officer James A Scott. The 63-year old Lala Lajpat Rai died as a result of the injuries sustained a few days later. This enraged many revolutionaries who vowed to avenge his death.

- Bhagat Singh and Rajguru shot another police officer John Saunders in a case of mistaken identity. They had intended to shoot Scott. However, the HSRA still claimed that revenge had been exacted.

- The next major activity of the HSRA was the Central Assembly bombing case. Bhagat Singh and BK Dutt bombed the Central Legislative Assembly, Delhi on 8th April 1929. Their only intention was to "make the deaf hear" and not to harm anyone. Nobody was injured in the bombing and both the revolutionaries courted arrest after the incident.

- As they were arrested, they shouted slogans like '**Inquilab Zindabad**' and '**Down with Imperialism**'.

- For this case, both Bhagat Singh and BK Dutt were sentenced to 'transportation for life'.

- In 1931, Bhagat Singh, Rajguru and Sukhdev were hanged to death for it.

- In 1929, the HSRA also bombed a train carrying the then viceroy of India, Lord Irwin. He was unharmed.

- Chandrasekhar Azad was also killed by the police in a shootout at Allahabad in 1931.

- After 1931, most leaders of the party had been killed or imprisoned. The party disintegrated as there was no leadership.

Chapter - 6

Bhagat Singh's Revolutionary Activities

Bhagat Singh's association with the revolutionaries began with Hindustan Republican Association(HRA). In 1927, he was first arrested on charges of association with the Kakori Conspiracy Case.

Kakori Conspiracy Case

The Kakori Conspiracy Case, also known as the **Kakori train robbery**, was the largest armed robbery in Indian history. Members of the Hindustan Socialist Republican Association (HSRA), Ram Prasad Bismil and Ashfaqullah Khan planned the robbery. This association was established to carry out revolutionary activities against the British rule with the objective of achieving independence. Since the association needed money for the purchase of firearms and weapons, Ram Prasad Bismil and his associates made a plan to rob a train on the Saharanpur Railway lines.

History of the Kakori Conspiracy

The robbery took place at Kakori, a village which was 16 kms to the north-west of Lucknow.On 9th August 1925, the **Number 8 Down Train** was travelling from Shahjahanpur to Lucknow. When it passed Kakori, one of the revolutionaries, Rajendra Lahiri pulled the emergency chain to stop the train. Subsequently, ten revolutionaries under the command of Ram Prasad Bismil stopped the train, disarmed the guards and passengers inside, busted open the guards' quarters safe, and stole the money. It is believed that they looted this specific train because it was carrying the money bags (taxes) which belonged to the Indians and was being transferred to the British government treasury. They looted only these bags (which were present in the guards' cabin and escaped to Lucknow.

Objectives of the Kakori Train Robbery

The objectives of this robbery were to:

- fund the HSRA with the money of British administration taxed from the Indians.
- to protest against the British administration collecting a lot of tax from Indians .
- obtain public attention by creating a positive image of the HSRA among Indians.

One lawyer, Ahmad Ali, who was a passenger, had got down to see his wife in the ladies compartment and was killed in an unintentional discharge by Manmathnath Gupta. Following the incident, the British administration arrested several of the revolutionaries who were members of the HSRA. Their leader, Ram Prasad Bismil was arrested at Shahjahanpur on 26th October 1925 and Ashfaqullah Khan was arrested on 7th December 1926 at Delhi. Sachindranath Sanyal, Rajendra Lahiri, and Jogesh Chandra Chatterjee had already been arrested in Bengal. Rajendra Lahiri was prosecuted in a Dakshineshwar bombing case.

Timeline of the Event

The train robbery was planned by Ram Prasad Bismil and Ashfaqullah Khan. Murari Lal, Rajendra Lahiri, Mukundi Lal Gupta, Sachindra Bakshi and Manmathnath Gupta were among the numerous revolutionaries who made up this association. The goal of the revolutionaries was to take over the guards' cabin, which contained money collected from various railway stations for deposit in Lucknow.

On September 26th 1925, British authorities detained Ram Prasad Bismil. The Kakori train incident trial proceeded at the Hamilton Session Court on May 21st 1926. In the middle of 1926, Ashfaqullah Khan and Sir Chandra Bakshi were detained following the conclusion of the proceedings.

Kakori Trial

Ram Prasad Bismil and others were charged with various offences, including robbery and murder. Fourteen people were released due to lack of evidence. Two of the accused – Ashfaqullah Khan and Sachindranath Bakshi were captured after the trial. Chandrashekhar Azad reorganized the HSRA in 1928 and operated it until his death in 27th February 1931.

Charges pressed against three men were dropped. Damodar Swarup Seth was discharged due to illness, while Veer Bhadra Tiwari and Jyoti Shankar Dixit were suspected of providing information to the authorities.

Two other individuals – Banarsi Lal and Indubhushan Mitra came to be approvers in return for a lenient sentence.

Court's Proceedings

Charges against 19 of the accused were withdrawn (2 had become approvers while 17 people had been released). The trial against the remaining 21 began on 1st May 1926 at the Special Sessions Court of Justice Archibald Hamilton. Abbas Salim Khan, Banwari Lal Bhargava, Gyan Chatterjee and Mohammad Ayuf were the assessors of the case. Of the 21 accused, two people namely Sachindranath Biswas and Lala Hargovind were released due to lack of evidence, while Gopi Mohan became an approver.

The court had appointed Jagat Narayan Mulla as public prosecutor knowingly; he had a prejudice against Ram Prasad Bismil since 1916, when Ram Prasad Bismil led the grand procession of Bal Gangadhar Tilak at Lucknow. He had also been the public prosecutor in the **Mainpuri Conspiracy Case** of 1918.

The government officers had also bribed many of the accused to become approvers. The trials were mainly based on the statements given by Banwari Lal who had met the revolutionaries and was also involved in planning the robbery activities taken up by the group at Bamrauli (25th December 1924), Bichpuri (9th March 1925) and Dwarikapur (25th May 1925). So, his statement was used as the main evidence to prove the HSRA members guilty.

The judgement of the case trials of Sessions Court was pronounced on 6th April 1927 as follows:

Ram Prasad Bismil, Roshan Singh and Rajendra Nath Lahiri were sentenced to death. Sachindranath Sanyal was given life imprisonment. Manmathnath Gupta was sentenced to 14 years' imprisonment. Jogesh Chandra Chatterjee, Govind Charan Kar, Raj Kumar Sinha, Ram Krishna Khatri and Mukundi Lal were sentenced to 10 years' imprisonment, while Suresh Chandra Bhattacharya and Vishnu Sharan Dublish were given 7 years' imprisonment. Bhupendra Nath Sanyal, Ram Dulare Trivedi, Prem Krishna Khanna and Pranawesh Chatterjee were sentenced to imprisonment for 5 years' and the least punishment (3 years' imprisonment) was given to Ram Nath Pandey and Banwari Lal.

Final Verdict

Following the arrest of Ashfaqullah Khan, the police interrogated him to try to gain supplementary evidence against his accomplices but he refused. Another supplementary case was filed against Ashfaqullah Khan and Sachindranath Bakshi in the court of Special Sessions Judge John Reginald William Bennett. An appeal was filed in the then Chief Court of Oudh (now Allahabad High Court – Lucknow Bench) on 18th July 1927. The case trials started the next day. The judgement of the trial was pronounced a month later on 11th August.

Hunger Strike in Jail

After the court gave the judgement of the main Kakori Conspiracy Case on 6th April 1927, a group photograph was taken and all the accused were sent to the different jails of the United Provinces. In the prisons, they were asked to wear jail uniforms like the other prisoners which lead to immediate protests and hunger strikes. The revolutionaries argued that since they had been charged with crimes against the British rule, they should be treated as political prisoners and thus should possess the rights and amenities provided to political prisoners.

Defense Committee

The legal defence for the arrested revolutionaries was provided by Govind Ballabh Pant, Mohan Lal Saxena, Chandra Bhanu Gupta, Ajit Prasad Jain, Gopi Nath Srivastava, R. M. Bahadurji, BK Chaudhury and Kripa Shankar Hajela.

Pandit Jagat Narayan Mulla, a leading advocate from Lucknow refused to defend the arrested revolutionaries. He was appointed as public prosecutor by the law of court.

Among the political figures who came out in support of those arrested for the Kakori train robbery were Motilal Nehru, Madan Mohan Malaviya, Muhammad Ali Jinnah, Lala Lajpat Rai, Jawaharlal Nehru , Ganesh Shankar Vidyarthi, Shiv Prasad Gupta, Shri Prakash and Acharya Narendra Dev.

Reaction in the Country

There were widespread protests against the court's decision all over the country. Members of the Central Legislature even petitioned the Viceroy of India to commute the death sentences given to the four men to life sentences. Appeals were also sent to the Privy Council. However, these requests were turned down and the young revolutionaries were finally executed. Appeals were claimed to have been also made by Mahatma Gandhi, despite his lack of executive authority.

Clemency Appeal

On 11th August 1927, the Chief Court endorsed the original judgement with an exception of one (7 yrs) punishment from the judgement of 6th April. A mercy appeal was filed in due course before the Provincial Governor of U.P. by the members of the legislative council which was dismissed. Ram Prasad Bismil wrote a letter to Madan Mohan Malaviya on 9th September 1927 from Gorakhpur jail. Malaviya sent a memorandum to the then Viceroy and Governor-General of India Lord Irwin with the signatures of 78 Members of Central Legislature, which was also turned down.

On 16th September 1927, the final mercy appeal was forwarded to Privy Council at London and to the King-Emperor through a famous lawyer of England, Henry S. L. Polak, but the British Government who had already decided to hang them, sent their final decision to the India office of Viceroy that all the four condemned prisoners were to be hanged till death on 19th December 1927.

Kakori Conspiracy Impact

At the time of the Kakori incident, everyone in India was aware of the country's need for freedom and was looking for alternate ways to achieve it. Some leaders, like Chandrashekhar Azad and Bhagat Singh, adopted this strategy, while others like Mahatma Gandhi, pursued the path of peace.

The intended attack actually had a much greater impact on the British empire than it may have appeared to have. Following the Kakori train robbery, the British government was the subject of numerous coordinated attacks. The executions of the rebels sparked protracted protests across the country. These small-scale organised protests and disruptions caused the empire's hold over India to quickly deteriorate, and it became very difficult for them to retain control over enraged India.

Kakori Conspiracy

The Kakori train robbery changed the way the system worked. Many young revolutionaries, including Sukhdev, Shiv Verma, and Jaidev Kapoor, set out to recognise HRA under the leadership of Chandrashekhar Azad.

The majority of the leading young revolutionaries from northern India finally gathered in Delhi on September 9th and 10th 1928, at the Feroz Shah Kotla Ground to form a new collective leadership, declare socialism as their main goal, and rename the Hindustan Republican Association as the Hindustan Socialist Republican Association. The Uttar Pradesh government has changed the appellation of the Kakori conspiracy to the Kakori train incident.

Chapter - 7

Lahore Conspiracy Case

On 17th December1927, Bhagat Singh and Shivaram Rajguru shot and killed **Assistant Superintendent of Police, John Saunders**. They were supported in this act by their compatriots Sukhdev Thapar and Chandrashekhar Azad. However, their original target was not Saunders but **Superintendent of Police, James Scott** who had ordered his men to lathi-charge protesters leading to the death of the nationalist leader, Lala Lajpat Rai.

Bhagat Singh along with few other revolutionaries like Shivram Rajguru, Chandrasekhar Azad and Sukhdev Thapar plotted a plan to assassinate James A Scott. In their agitated mind to kill James A Scott, they mistook J. P Saunders as James A Scott and killed him on December 17th 1928. J. P. Saunders was assistant Superintendent of Police. On knowing his mistake fearing arrest Bhagat Singh left Lahore.

How this all happened is narrated below?

In 1928, the British government set up the Simon Commission to report on the political situation in India. Some Indian political parties boycotted the Commission because there were no Indian members in it. Soon there were protests across the country. When the Commission visited Lahore on 30th October 1928, Lala Lajpat Rai led a march in protest against it. The attempts by the police to disperse the large crowd resulted in violence. The Superintendent of Police, James A. Scott, ordered the police to lathi charge the protesters and personally assaulted Lala Lajpat Rai who was injured. Lala Lajpat Rai succumbed to injuries on 17th November 1928. The doctors thought that his death might have been hastened by the blows and injuries he had received. When the matter was raised in the Parliament of the United Kingdom, the British Government denied any role in Lala Lajpat Rai's death.

Bhagat Singh was an active member of the **Hindustan Republican Association (HRA)** and was largely responsible for its change of name to **Hindustan Socialist Republican Association (HSRA)** in 1928. The HSRA vowed to avenge Lala Lajpat Rai's death. Bhagat Singh conspired with other revolutionaries like Shivaram Rajguru, Sukhdev Thapar and Chandrashekhar Azad to kill Scott. However, in a case of mistaken identity, the revolutionaries shot **John P. Saunders**, an Assistant Superintendent of Police, as he was leaving the District Police Headquarters in Lahore on 17th December 1928.

The **Naujawan Bharat Sabha** which had organised the Lahore protest march along with the HSRA, found that attendance at its subsequent public meetings dropped sharply. Politicians, activists, and newspapers, including **The People**, which Lala Lajpat Rai had founded in 1925, stressed that non-cooperation was preferable to violence. The murder was condemned as a retrograde action by Mahatma Gandhi, the Congress leader, but Jawaharlal Nehru later wrote that:

"Bhagat Singh did not become popular because of his act of terrorism but because he seemed to vindicate, for the moment, the honour of Lala Lajpat Rai, and through him of the nation. He became a symbol, the act was forgotten, the symbol remained, and within a few months each town and village of the Punjab, and to a lesser extent in the rest of northern India, resounded with his name. Innumerable songs grew about him and the popularity that the man achieved was something amazing."

Bhagat Singh and his revolutionary friends decided to avenge the death of the dear leader. However, in a case of mistaken identity, they assassinated another police official J P Saunders. This was also known as the **Lahore Conspiracy Case**.

Chapter - 8

Lahore Conspiracy Case contd....

Killing of Channan Singh

After killing John P. Saunders, the group escaped through the D.A.V. College entrance, across the road from the District Police Headquarters. **Channan Singh**, a Head Constable who was chasing them, was shot dead by Chandrashekhar Azad. They then fled on bicycles to pre-arranged safe houses. The police launched a massive search operation to catch them, blocking all entrances and exits to and from the city; the CID kept a watch on all young men leaving Lahore. The fugitives hid for the next two days.

On 19th December 1928, Sukhdev called on Durgawati Devi, also known as Durga Bhabhi, wife of another HSRA member, Bhagwati Charan Vohra, for help, which she agreed to provide. They decided to catch the train departing from Lahore to Bathinda en route to Howrah (Calcutta) early the next morning.

With the help of Durgawati Devi Bhagat Singh left Lahore and went to Howrah. To hide his identity Bhagat Singh shaved his beard and cut his hair and wore a hat even though it was against the principles of Sikhism.

Escape of Bhagat Singh from Lahore

Bhagat Singh and Rajguru, both carrying loaded revolvers, left the house early the next day. Dressed in western attire (Bhagat Singh cut his hair, shaved his beard and wore a hat over cropped hair), and carrying Devi's sleeping child, Bhagat Singh and Devi passed as a young couple, while Rajguru carried their luggage as their servant. At the station, Bhagat Singh managed to conceal his identity while buying tickets, and the three boarded the train heading to Cawnpore (now Kanpur). There they boarded a train for Lucknow since the CID at Howrah railway station usually scrutinised passengers on the direct train from Lahore. At Lucknow, Rajguru left separately for Benares while Bhagat Singh, Devi and the infant went to Howrah, with all except Bhagat Singh returning to Lahore a few days later.

Chapter - 9

Central Assembly Bombing Case

To protest against the **Public Safety Bill** and **Trade Dispute Act,** Bhagat Singh and few other members thought to explode bomb inside the Central Legislative Assembly from the Visitors' Gallery. Their intention was not to hurt or kill anyone from the bombing. On 8th April 1929, Bhagat Singh along with Batukeshwar Dutt threw three bombs on the corridors of the assembly by throwing leaflets They shouted slogans of **"Inquilab Zindabad"** during the whole arrest. The slogan became quite popular among the youth and many freedom fighters.

The smoke filled the assembly but still Bhagat Singh and Batukeshwar Dutt did not escape from the scene. Both the revolutionaries did not resist arrest since they wanted to spread their message of revolution and anti-imperialism and wanted to use the trial as a platform for it.

There were no causalities in the incident as it was never their intention to cause physical harm to anyone. Their aim was 'to make the deaf hear'.

Bhagat Singh was the mastermind behind the incident and was inspired by **Auguste Vaillant**, a French anarchist, who was executed by France for a similar incident in Paris.

In the trial for the incident, both Bhagat Singh and Batukeshwar Dutt were sentenced to imprisonment for life.

By this time Bhagat Singh was also linked to the J P Saunder's murder incident. He, along with Rajguru and Sukhdev was charged with the murder of Saunders.

Chapter - 10

Trial of Bhagat Singh

The trial began in May 1929. Although Batukeshwar Dutt had Afsar Ali as his counsel, Bhagat Singh preferred to defend himself. He made the stand of the revolutionaries clear, saying – **'Force when aggressively applied is violence and therefore is unjustifiable, but when used for the furtherance of a legitimate cause it has its moral justification.'** As expected, the court did not rule in favour of the revolutionaries terming their action as 'malicious and unlawful intent'.

The young revolutionaries started a hunger strike in Lahore prison demanding better conditions for political prisoners who were also treated as criminals.

They were met by many leaders including Jawaharlal Nehru while they fasted for 116 days which only ended after repeated requests from family and Congress leaders.

But the trial was a one-sided affair and Bhagat Singh, Sukhdev, and Rajguru were sentenced to death. The verdict was met with large criticism and many national leaders requested to reduce the sentence but in vain.

The three were ordered to be hanged on 24th March 1931 but the sentence was carried out a day earlier at the Lahore jail.

The executions were reported widely by the press, especially as they took place on the eve of the annual convention of the Congress Party in Karachi. Gandhi faced black flag demonstrations by angry youths who shouted: **"Down with Gandhi."**

Chapter - 11

Execution of Bhagat Singh

The trial proceedings started against all the 28 accused and arrested. Finally the court ordered for the execution of Bhagat Singh, Shivaram Rajguriu and Sukhdev Thapar in **Lahore Conspiracy Case**. On 23rd March 1931 at 7:30 am Bhagat Singh was hanged to death in Lahore jail along with his other inmates Rajguru and Sukhdev. The execution was supervised by the honorary Judge who also signed the three death warrants. It is believed that even while going to the gallows all the three were cheerfully singing slogans like **'down with British imperialism' and 'Inquilab Zindabad'**.. Later the dead bodies of the three were secretly cremated at the Hussainiwala located beside the river Sutlej.

There was severe criticism in the way the trial and execution of Bhagat Singh happened. The Supreme Court described it as "contrary to the fundamental doctrine of criminal jurisprudence." The accused was not given an opportunity to defend his case and also the judgement was passed ex parte.

Chapter - 12

Individual Heroism vs Mass Movement

Bhagat Singh initially believed in individual heroism to achieve the goal. However, he later realised that individual heroism stood no chance against the brutal force of the British empire and the only way to a successful revolution was to unleash a popular broad-based movement.

Bhagat Singh was a follower and admirer of Marxism and was inspired by the writings of Vlaimir Lenin, Leon Trotsky and Mikhail Bakunin.

On 15th August 2008, an 18-foot tall bronze statue of Singh was installed in the Parliament of India, next to the statues of Indira Gandhi and Subhas Chandra Bose. A portrait of Bhagat Singh and Batukeshwar Dutt also adorns the walls of the Parliament House.

Chapter - 13

Legacy and Memorials of Bhagat Singh

Every year, March 23rd is observed as **Martyrs' Day** as a tribute to freedom fighters Bhagat Singh, Sukhdev Thapar, and Shivaram Rajguru. The day is also known as **Shaheed Diwas** or **Sarvodaya Day.**

During the centenary of his birth, a group of intellectuals set-up an institution named **Bhagat Singh Sansthan** to commemorate him and his ideals.

He was an atheist and an ardent reader. His book, **"Why I am an Athiest"** is quite popular.

During his early period of revolutionary, Bhagat Singh influenced youth and other Indians with his writings against the British and also on its policies. This influenced a lot of youths and the Indians to oppose British in all its activities which led to huge disruption. Considering his influence on the youth Bhagat Singh was also arrested and was later released after five long days with a bond of 60,000 Rs.

To fight against the British was in the blood of Bhagat Singh. The British government introduced **Simon Commission** in the year 1928. There was a nation-wide strike against the Simon Commission and Sir Simon was welcomed to India with black flags. There was a massive protest against the Simon Commission by shouting slogans like **'Go back Simon.'** On 30th October, 1928 Lala Lajpat Rai led the protest against the Simon Commission. Thousands of people had gathered to protest against the Simon Commission which resulted in violent acts.

To disperse the crowd and to take control of the situation, Superintendent of Police, James A Scott ordered the police officers to do lathi charge on the crowd. During the lathi charge Lala Lajpat Rai was severely injured and died . Bhagat Singh had great respect for Lala Lajpat Rai. Hence, he vowed to take revenge on the British for his death.

Bhagat Singh remains a significant figure in Indian iconography to the present day. His memory, however, defies categorisation and presents problems for various groups that might try to appropriate it. Pritam Singh, a professor who has specialised in the study of federalism, nationalism and development in India, notes that:

"Bhagat Singh represents a challenge to almost every tendency in Indian politics. Gandhi-inspired Indian nationalists, Hindu nationalists, Sikh nationalists, the parliamentary Left and the pro-armed struggle Naxalite Left compete with each other to appropriate the legacy of Bhagat Singh, and yet each one of them is faced with a contradiction in making a claim to his legacy. Gandhi-inspired Indian nationalists find Bhagat Singh's resort to violence problematic, the Hindu and Sikh nationalists find his atheism troubling, the parliamentary Left finds his ideas and actions as more close to the perspective of the Naxalites and the Naxalites find Bhagat Singh's critique of individual terrorism in his later life an uncomfortable historical fact."

- On 15th August 2008, an 18-foot tall bronze statue of Singh was installed in the Parliament of India, next to the statues of Indira Gandhi and Subhas Chandra Bose. A portrait of Bhagat Singh and Batukeshwar Dutt also adorns the walls of the Parliament House.

- The National Martyrs Memorial, built at Hussainiwala in memory of Bhagat Singh, Sukhdev and Rajguru.

- The place where Singh was cremated, at Hussainiwala on the banks of the Sutlej river, became a Pakistani territory during the partition. On 17th January 1961, it was transferred to India in exchange for 12 villages near the Sulemanki Headworks. Batukeshwar Dutt was cremated there on 19th July 1965 in accordance with his last wishes. The National Martyrs Memorial was built on the cremation spot in 1968 and has memorials of Singh, Rajguru and Sukhdev. During the 1971 India–Pakistan war, the memorial was damaged and the statues of the martyrs were removed by the Pakistani Army. They have not been returned but the memorial was rebuilt in 1973.

- The **Shaheedi Mela** (Punjabi: Martyrdom Fair) is an event held annually on 23rd March when people pay homage at the National Martyrs Memorial. The day is also observed across the Indian state of Punjab.

- The **Shaheed-e-Azam Sardar Bhagat Singh Museum** opened on the 50th anniversary of his death at his ancestral village, Khatkar Kalan.

Exhibits include Bhagat Singh's ashes, the blood-soaked sand, and the blood-stained newspaper in which the ashes were wrapped. A page of the first Lahore Conspiracy Case's judgement in which Kartar Singh Sarabha was sentenced to death and on which Singh put some notes is also displayed, as well as a copy of the Bhagavad Gita with Bhagat Singh's signature, which was given to him in the Lahore Jail, and other personal belongings.

- The **Bhagat Singh Memorial** was built in 2009 in Khatkar Kalan at a cost of ₹168 million (US$2.1 million).

- The **Supreme Court of India** established a museum to display landmarks in the history of India's judicial system, displaying records of some historic trials. The first exhibition that was organised was the Trial of Bhagat Singh, which opened on 28 September 2007, on the centenary celebrations of Singh's birth.

Chapter - 14

Bhagat Singh's Popularity

Bhagat Singh was a follower of Kartar Singh Sarabha who was the founder of **Ghadar Party.** Singh was attracted towards anarchism and communism. Even though Bhagat Singh believed in Marxist ideas he never joined any communist party. When Gandhiji called off the Non-Cooperation there was huge riots between Hindus and Muslims. Seeing this and understanding how people were fighting for religion instead against the British, Bhagat Singh started to disbelieve all the religious beliefs and started to read books of Lenin and Trotsky.

Bhagat Singh became an inspiration to thousands of youth who came forward to fight against the British for their motherland.

Subhas Chandra Bose said that, **"Bhagat Singh had become the symbol of new awakening among the youths."**

Jawaharlal Nehru also said that, **"He was a clean and honest fighter who faced the enemy in the open field with lot of courage. He was like a spark that became a flame in a short time and spread from one end of the country to the other dispelling the prevailing darkness everywhere."**

Bhagat Singh was cremated at Hussainiwala on the banks of river Sutlej. After India and Pakistan partitioned in 1947 the village went into the Pakistan borders. In the year 1961, India got the village back by exchanging it with 12 other villages to Pakistan. In 1968, a **Martyrs Memorial** was built at the cremation spot. It also has memorials of Bhagat Singh, Rajguru and Sukhdev. During the India-Pakistan war in the year 1971 the memorial was damaged by the Pakistani army. It was again rebuilt in the year 1973.

The **Bhagat Singh Memorial** was built in Khatar Kalan in the year 2009.

Chapter - 15

Quotes of Bhagat Singh

Shaheed Bhagat Singh, the greatest freedom fighter inspires thousands of Indians across generations for his courage. The British administrators dreaded the freedom fighter trio - Bhagat Singh, Rajguru and Sukhdev - for their bravery. They were sentenced to death in the Lahore Conspiracy Case for killing British police officer, John Saunders.

Bhagat Singh's memorable quotes to remember.

- "They may kill me, but they cannot kill my ideas. They can crush my body, but they will not be able to crush my spirit."

- "Revolution is an inalienable right of mankind. Freedom is an imperishable birth right of all."

- "I am such a lunatic that I am free even in jail."

- "I am full of ambition and hope and charm of life. But I can renounce everything at the time of need."

- "If the deaf have to hear, the sound has to be very loud."

- "Merciless criticism and independent thinking are two traits of revolutionary thinking. Lovers, lunatics and poets are made of the same stuff."

- "One should not interpret the word 'revolution' in its literal sense. Various meanings and significance are attributed to this word, according to the interests of those who use or misuse it. For the established agencies of exploitation it conjures up a feeling of blood-stained horror. To the revolutionaries, it is a sacred phrase."

- "Bombs and pistols don't make a revolution. The sword of revolution is sharpened on the whetting stone of ideas.

- "Labour is the real sustainer of society."
- "People get accustomed to the established order of things and tremble at the idea of change. It is this lethargic spirit that needs be replaced by the revolutionary spirit."

Chapter - 16

Revolutionaries in the Indian Freedom Movement

Shivaram Rajguru

Shivaram Rajguru (1908-1931) was a great Indian freedom fighter who played a major role in the India's struggle for Independence. He is amongst those great Indian revolutionaries who sacrificed their lives for the freedom of our country. His full name was Hari Shivaram.He was born into a Deshastha Brahmin family. Since his childhood days, he had witnessed the brutal atrocities that the Imperial British Raj inflicted on India and her people. This instilled within him a strong urge to join hands with the revolutionaries in a bid for India's freedom struggle.

In the days of the Indian Freedom Movement, the **Hindustan Socialist Republican Army (HSRA)** was an active force working against the British. Their main motive was to strike fear into the heart of the British regime. They simultaneously spread awareness amongst the people. They made them take notice of the growing domestic uprising when they dealt crucial blows with attacks like in the **Lahore Conspiracy Case** (December 18, 1928) and the bombing of the **Central Assembly Hall** in New Delhi (April 8, 1929).

The protest against the Simon Commission in October 1928 saw the British police lathi-charge the protestors, severely injuring veteran leader Lala Lajpat Rai. Owing to the excessive beating, Lala succumbed to his injuries, which thus instilled revenge in the hearts of the revolutionaries. On December 18th 1928, in Ferozepur, Lahore, a planned retaliation was enforced that led to the assassination of Deputy Superintendent of Police, J.P. Saunders. Shivaram Rajguru, along with Sukhdev Thapar, was accomplice of the legendary Bhagat Singh who spearheaded the attack. Rajguru then went into hiding in Nagpur. Whilst taking shelter in the house of an RSS worker, he even met Dr. K B Hedgewar. On his travel to

Pune, however, Shivaram was finally arrested. Bhagat Singh, Shivaram Rajguru and Sukhdev Thapar were then convicted of their crime and sentenced to death.

On March 23rd 1931, the three brave revolutionaries were hanged, whilst their bodies were cremated on the banks of the River Sutlej. Shivaram Rajguru was only 23 years old when he became a martyr; however, he will always be remembered in the pages of Indian history for his valour and dedication of his life towards India's independence.

Sukhdev Thapar

Sukhdev Thapar is one of the most respected revolutionaries who fought for India's freedom, and yet, little is known about him . Sukhdev was born on 15th May 1907 in Naughara village in Ludhiana, Punjab. His father, Sri Ramlila Thapar, a small businessman, passed away when Sukhdev was three-years-old. Young Sukhdev grew up in Lyallpur under the guardianship of his uncle, Sri Achintram Thapar who was a prominent member of civil society, a freedom fighter, and a member of the Arya Samaj. Sukhdev was only twelve years old when his uncle was arrested by the British police for organizing an agitation against the **Rowlatt Act**. This incident impacted Sukhdev, and his resentment towards the British authorities just grew. The arrest of his uncle again in 1921 during the **Non-Cooperation Movement** was the final nail in the coffin. It enraged him to such an extent that he was determined to make the authorities pay for their indiscriminate use of the law.

Sukhdev's involvement in India's freedom struggle can be traced to Lahore, where he was studying in the National College, which happened to be a centre of nationalist politics. While in college, for a brief period Sukhdev became a member of the **Satyagraha League** that was affiliated with the Indian National Congress. Later, Sukhdev came in contact with Bhagat Singh, Bhagwati Charan Vohra, Yashpal, and others who were associated with the revolutionary organization that was originally called the **Hindustan Republican Association (HRA)**. coordinator for HRA in Punjab was his college Professor Jaichandra Vidyalankar. It is through them that Sukhdev was introduced to the revolutionary movement.

In 1926, Bhagat Singh, Sukhdev, Bhagwati Charan Vohra, and others formed the **Naujawan Bharat Sabha**. Sukhdev was elected to the committee of this organization. In the years to come, the responsibility of running the organization fell upon his shoulders as both Bhagat Singh and Bhagwati Charan Vohra got involved in reviving the revolutionary movement.

When the Hindustan Republican Association transitioned into the Hindustan Socialist Republican Association (HSRA), Sukhdev was elected to its central committee and given charge of the Punjab region. Under his leadership, the HSRA grew exponentially in Punjab. Sukhdev was cautious and took many precautions while recruiting new members to the revolutionary party.

Meanwhile, the HSRA deputed Batukeshwar Dutt and Bejoy Kumar Sinha to throw low-grade smoke bombs in the Central Legislative Assembly to protest against the proposed **Trade Dispute Bill** and the Public Safety Bill. Although Sukhdev was present during the meeting, he hardly uttered a word. After the meeting was over, it is said, he got into a heated dispute with Bhagat Singh and compelled him to lead the assignment. Sukhdev's argument was that once the revolutionaries were caught, the world had to be convinced about their intent, and he felt only Bhagat Singh had the ability and power to present the ideas and programs of the revolutionaries globally. Bhagat Singh acceded to his plea, and at his behest, the central committee of the HSRA reconvened and paved the way for him to lead the attack in what came to be known as the **Assembly Bomb Case.**

Bhagat Singh and Batukeshwar Dutt were caught and tried in the Assembly Bomb Case. In the course of the investigations, it was found that Bhagat Singh, along with Sukhdev and Rajguru, were the men behind the murder of Colonel J P Saunders, whom they had shot, mistaking him for the police officer who had ordered the lathi-charge in which Lala Lajpat Rai had sustained fatal injuries. This case was reopened, and Bhagat Singh, Rajguru, and Sukhdev were charged with the murder of Saunders.

The fearless and defiant attitude of the revolutionaries was reported in the newspapers. According to reports, they would enter the courtroom shouting slogans like 'Inquilab Zindabad', 'Long Live the Proletariat' and singing songs such as 'Sarfaroshi ki tamanna ab hamare dil mei hai' ("our heart is filled with the desire for martyrdom"). Sukhdev and his comrades went on a hunger strike to protest against the inhuman conditions in the jail. They demanded that they be treated as political prisoners and not as criminals. The entire nation was stirred and rallied behind these revolutionaries. However, the courts convicted them and on 23rd March 1931, Sukhdev was hanged in Lahore Jail along with Bhagat Singh and Rajguru. The nation commemorates this day as **Shaheed Diwas** (Martyr's Day) to honour their selfless sacrifice for the freedom of the country.

Chandrashekhar Azad

Chandrashekhar Tiwari who was popularly known as Chandrashekhar Azad was an Indian Revolutionary leader and a freedom fighter. After the deaths of the founder of **Hindustan Republican Association (HRA)**, Ram Prasad Bismil, and three other prominent party leaders, Roshan Singh, Rajendra Nath Lahiri, and Ashfaqulla Khan, he reorganized the Hindustan Republican Association (HRA) under the new name of Hindustan Socialist Republican Association (HSRA). When signing pamphlets as the commander in chief of the HSRA, he often used the alias **"Balraj."**

Chandrashekhar Azad: Early Life, Family and Education

- Chandrashekhar Azad was born on 23rd July 1906.

- Chandrasekhar Azad's birthplace is the present-day Alirajpur district of Madhya Pradesh.

- His real name was Chandra Shekhar Tiwari.

- Chandrasekhar Azad's father's name was Sitaram Tiwari and his mother's name was Jagrani Devi.

- He received his early education at Bhavra.

- Later, he went to Kashi Vidyapeeth, Banaras for higher education.

- At a young age, Chandrasekhar Azad became involved in revolutionary activities. In 1921 he joined the **non-cooperation movement** started by Mahatma Gandhi to protest against the **Jallianwala Bagh massacre**.

- He was imprisoned for the first time when he was captured by Britishers at the age of 15 and sentenced to 15 lashes.

- Following this incident, he took the surname Azad and became known as Chandrashekhar Azad.

Revolutionary Activities of Chandrashekhar Azad

- Mahatma Gandhi suspended the Non-Cooperation movement in February 1922 as a result of the Chauri-Chaura incident, which was a blow to Azad's Nationalist sentiments.

- He then determined that a massive approach would be more effective in achieving his goal.

- During this time he met a lot of young Revolutionary Leaders of India.

- Ram Prasad Bismil, Jogesh Chandra Chatterjee, Sachindra Nath Sanyal, Shachindra Nath Bakshi, and Ashfaqulla Khan formed the Hindustan Republican Association in 1923.

- Chandra Shekhar Azad met Manmath Nath Gupta, a young revolutionary who introduced him to Ram Prasad Bismil, the founder of the Hindustan Republican Association (HRA), a revolutionary group.

- He then became a member of the Hindustan Republican Association and began fundraising for it. Robberies of government property are used to collect the rest of the funds.

- He was involved in the Kakori Train Robbery that happened in 1925. In the year 1928, he shot J.P. Saunders to take revenge of Lala Lajpat Rai's murder in Lahore. Also, he had attempted to blow away India's Viceroy's train in 1929.

- The British clamped down on revolutionary movements in the wake of the Kakori train robbery in 1925.

- Prasad, Ashfaqulla Khan, Thakur Roshan Singh, and Rajendra Nath Lahiri were all found guilty and sentenced to death.

- Azad, Keshab Chakravarthy, and Murari Sharma managed to escape being apprehended.

- Later, with the aid of revolutionaries including Sheo Verma and Mahaveer Singh, Chandra Shekhar Azad reorganized the HRA.

- Azad and Bhagat Singh secretly renamed the Hindustan Republican Association (HRA) as the Hindustan Socialist Republican Association (HSRA) on September 9, 1928 to achieve their primary goal of a socialist-based independent India.

- For a time, Azad made Jhansi the headquarters of his HRA organisation. He practiced shooting in the forest of Orchha, 15 kilometers from Jhansi, and, as an expert marksman, he also taught other members of his tribe.

- For a long time, he lived in a hut near a Hanuman temple on the banks of the Satar River under the alias of Pandit Harishankar Bramhachari.

- He developed a good relationship with the local residents by teaching children from the nearby village of Dharampura.

- He learned to drive a car at the Bundelkhand Motor Garage in Sadar Bazar while living in Jhansi.

- Sadashivrao Malkapurkar, Vishwanath Vaishampayan, and Bhagwan Das Mahaur became close friends with him and joined his revolutionary party.

- Azad was also loyal to the then-congress leaders Raghunath Vinayak Dhulekar and Sitaram Bhaskar Bhagwat.

- He also stayed at Rudra Narayan Singh's house in Nai Basti and Bhagwat's house in Nagra for a while.

- Bundelkhand was one of his most devoted supporters. Dewan Kesri Shatrughan Singh, the father of the Bundelkhand freedom movement, aided Azad financially as well as with arms and fighters. Azad paid numerous visits to his fort in Mangrauth.

Chandrasekhar Azad and Bhagat Singh

The Hindustan Republican Association (HRA) was created by Jogesh Chandra Chatterjee, Bismil, Sachindra Nath Bakshi, Sachindra Nath Sanyal in 1923. After the Kakori train robbery in 1925, the Britishers attempted to suppress revolutionaries. Ashfaqulla Khan, Prasad, Rajendra Nath Lahiri, and Thakur Roshan Singh were sentenced to death for their participation in the revolutionary activities.

Murari Lal Gupta, Chakravarthy, Azad and Keshab evaded capture. With the help of revolutionaries like Mahavir Singh and Shiv Verma, Chandrashekhar Azad reorganized the association.

Azad along with Bhagat Singh and other revolutionaries secretly restructured the Hindustan Republican Association (HRA) in 1928 and renamed it the Hindustan Socialist Republican Association (HSRA) on 8-9 September in order to achieve their primary goal of an independent India based on the idea of socialism.

The revolutionary activities of Azad are described by Manmath Nath Gupta, a member of HSRA in his multiple writings. Gupta has also dedicated a section in his book "History of the Indian Revolutionary Movement" to describe the works of Azad. He named this section "Chandrashekhar Azad."

Chandrashekhar Azad's Death

After being surrounded by police and finding no way out after the ammunition ran out, Chandra Shekhar Azad shot himself and died on 27 February 1931 at Alfred Park which is now famously known as Azad Park in Allahabad.

After Veerbhadra Tiwari, their old companion who later turned traitor told them of his presence in the park, the police surrounded him.

In the course of defending himself, he was wounded, and Sukhdev Raj killed three police officers and injured others. Sukhdev Raj was able to flee as a result of his actions.

Without telling the general public, the body was taken to Rasulabad Ghat for cremation. People crowded the park where the incident occurred as soon as word got out. They chanted anti-British slogans and thanked Azad.

Chandrashekhar Azad's Quotes

Some of the famous Chandra Shekhar Azad slogans during the Indian Independence movement were as follows:

- "Aisi jawaani kisi kaam ki nahi jo apni matra bhoomi ke kaam na aa sake."
- "Ab bhi jiska khoon na khaula khoon nahi wo pani hai, jo desh ke kaam na aaye woh bekar jawani hai (If yet your blood does not rage, then it is water that flows in your veins. For what is the flush of youth if it is not of service to the motherland)."
- "Don't see others doing better than you, beat your own records every day because success is a fight between you and yourself."
- "I believe in a religion that propagates freedom, equality and brotherhood."
- "A plane is always safe on the ground, but it is not made for that. Always take some meaningful risks in life to achieve great heights."

Chandrashekhar Azad's Legacy

Many schools, roads, colleges, and other public institutes in India are named after him. Starting from Jagdish Gautam's film **Chandrashekhar Azad** released in 1963 and Manoj Kumar's film **Shaheed** in 1965, many films have portrayed the character of Azad. The Bollywood actor Manmohan portrayed Azad in a 1965 film. Sunny Deol played his character in the movie **23 March 1931: Shaheed**. Akhilendra Mishra also played Azad in the movie **The Legend of Bhagat Singh** and Raj Zutshi played Azad in the movie **Shaheed-e-Azam**. In the film, **Rang De Basanti** directed and produced by Rakesh Om Prakash Mehra, Aamir Khan portrayed Azad.

Jawaharlal Nehru writes in his autobiography that he met Azad a few weeks before his death, discussing the impact of the Gandhi-Irwin pact.

Nehru saw the futility of Azad's methods and was not completely convinced by his peaceful methods.

The lives of **Bhagat Singh, Rajguru, Azad** and **Ashfaq** were depicted in the film Rang De Basanti released in 2006 in which Aamir Khan portrayed Azad. The movie described the lives of these young revolutionaries so today's youth can take inspiration from them.

The 2018 television series **Chandrashekhar** displayed the journey of Chandrashekhar Azad from a young boy to a revolutionary leader. In this series, Ayaan Zubair portrayed the early life of Azad, Dev Joshi played Azad in his teens and Karan Sharma played adult Azad.

Conclusion

Chandrashekhar Azad was known for his organizational abilities, and he was instrumental in the **Hindustan Socialist Republican Association's** reorganization. In either case, he desired full independence for India. To avenge Lala Lajpat Rai's murder, he assassinated British Assistant Superintendent of Police John P Saunders. He became a wanted man as a result of his crimes, but he was able to elude the cops for several years. He was Bhagat Singh's mentor. One of his friends betrayed him, and the British police seized him. He fought valiantly, but when he saw no other way out, he shot himself to keep his promise of not being captured alive.

Ram Prasad Bismil

"Desh hit paida huye hai

Desh par marr jayenge

Marte marte desh ko

zinda magar kar jayenge."

Ram Prasad Bismil got his name etched as a prominent freedom fighter with his participation in the **Mainpuri conspiracy** of 1918. Bismil along with Genda Lal Dixit, a school teacher from Auraiya, organised youth from Etahwah, Mainpuri, Agra and Shahjahanpur districts to strengthen their organisations, **'Matrivedi'** and **'Shivaji Samiti'**. He published a pamphlet titled **'Deshwasiyon ke Naam'** and distributed it along with his poem **'Mainpuri ki Pratigya'** on January 28th 1918. To collect funds for the parties, they looted government coffers.

His ideals of freedom struggle stood in stark contrast to that of Mahatma Gandhi and he would reportedly say "independence would not be achieved by means of non-violence". After conflicting views and growing resentment with the Congress party, he formed the Hindustan Republic Association which soon had leaders like Bhagat Singh and Chandrashekhar Azad.

On August 9th 1925, Ram Prasad Bismil along with companions Ashfaqulla Khan and others executed the plan of looting the train at Kakori near Lucknow. After the revolutionaries stopped the 8-Down Saharanpur Lucknow passenger train at Kakori, Ashfaqullah Khan, Sachindra Bakshi, Rajendra Lahiri and Ram Prasad Bismil subdued the guard and looted cash meant for the treasury. Within a month of the attack, the angered colonial authorities arrested more than a dozen HRA members.After the trial in the so-called **Kakori conspiracy**, these four revolutionaries were sentenced to death.

Ashfaqulla Khan

Ashfaqulla Khan was born in the Shahjahanpur district of the United Provinces. He was the youngest among his five siblings.

In 1918, while he was in the seventh standard, police raided his school and arrested a student Rajaram Bhartiya in relation to the **Mainpuri Conspiracy**, in which activists organised looting in Mainpuri to fund the publication of anti-colonial literature. The arrest spurred his engagement in revolutionary activities in the United Provinces.

Ashfaqulla Khan met Ram Prasad Bismil, a revolutionary who was closely involved in the Mainpuri Conspiracy, through a friend. He soon became closely tied to Bismil and joined him in activities related to non-cooperation, the Swaraj Party, and the Hindustan Republican Association. Bismil and Khan were also both poets, with Khan writing Urdu poetry under the pseudonym **Hasrat**.

Like others in the Hindustan Republican Association, Khan was strongly inspired by Lenin and the Bolshevik Revolution in Russia. He expressed beliefs in the liberation of the poor and the rejection of capitalist interests. He also spoke against religious communalism, identifying it as a British tool to control the Indian population and prevent Indian independence.

Involvement in the Kakori train robbery

The revolutionaries of the Hindustan Republican Association organised a meeting in Shahjahanpur on 8th August 1925 to determine how to raise funds for arms and ammunition. They decided to rob a train carrying government cash through Kakori. The HRA had previously executed similar train robberies, inspired by the Russian Bolshevik technique of using robbery to fund revolutionary operations. He was originally against the Kakori train robbery, but eventually agreed to participate when others in the HRA expressed approval of the plan.

On 9th August 1925, Khan and other revolutionaries, namely Ram Prasad Bismil, Rajendra Lahiri, Thakur Roshan Singh, Sachindra Bakshi, Chandrashekhar Azad, Keshab Chakravarty, Banwari Lal, Murari Lal Gupta, Mukundi Lal, and Manmathnath Gupta, attacked and robbed a government train in Kakori near Lucknow. After the robbery, the British government launched an extensive investigative campaign to catch the perpetrators. On the morning of 26th October 1925, Bismil was caught by the police. Khan fled to Nepal to evade capture. From Nepal, he travelled to Kanpur and then Daltonganj, where he worked as a clerk at an engineering firm under a pseudonym.

Capture and Trial

Eventually, Khan decided to travel to Delhi to continue his revolutionary activities. While in Delhi, he met with a Pathan friend he had known in Shahjahanpur, who secretly reported his whereabouts to the police. On the morning of 7th December 1926, Khan was captured and arrested by the Delhi Police. He was detained in the District Jail at Faizabad and a case was filed against him.

The trial of the Kakori train robbers was held for over a year in Lucknow. The HRA had released an official statement in 1925 claiming that they did not consider themselves terrorists and instead saw their revolutionary activities as a way to fight back against the violence of the colonial government. While in prison, Khan wrote a letter that expressed a similar sentiment, confirming that he did not aim to spread violence through the HRA but only hoped to ensure India's independence.

Death and Aftermath

The case for the Kakori robbery was concluded by imposing the death sentence on Bismil, Khan, Lahiri, and Roshan. The others were given life sentences. Khan was sentenced to death by hanging and executed on 19th December 1927 at the Faizabad jail. He is considered a martyr for the cause of India's independence.

After the hangings of Khan, Bismil, Lahiri and Roshan, the HRA changed their name to the Hindustan Socialist Republican Army and began officially espousing socialist and Marxist ideologies.

Chapter - 17

Reactions to the Executions

The executions were reported widely by the press, especially as they took place on the eve of the annual convention of the Congress party at Karachi. Gandhi faced black flag demonstrations by angry youths who shouted **"Down with Gandhi."**

The **New York Times** reported:

"A reign of terror in the city of Cawnpore in the United Provinces and an attack on Mahatma Gandhi by a youth outside Karachi were among the answers of the Indian extremists today to the hanging of Bhagat Singh and two fellow-assassins."

Hartals and strikes of mourning were called. The **Congress party**, during the Karachi session, declared:

"While dissociating itself from and disapproving of political violence in any shape or form, this Congress places on record its admiration of the bravery and sacrifice of Bhagat Singh, Sukhdev and Rajguru and mourns with their bereaved families the loss of these lives. The Congress is of the opinion that their triple execution was an act of wanton vengeance and a deliberate flouting of the unanimous demand of the nation for commutation. This Congress is further of the opinion that the [British] Government lost a golden opportunity for promoting good-will between the two nations, admittedly held to be crucial at this juncture, and for winning over to methods of peace a party which, driven to despair, resorts to political violence."

In the issue of **Young India** of 29th March 1931, Gandhiji wrote:

"Bhagat Singh and his two associates have been hanged. The Congress made many attempts to save their lives and the Government entertained many hopes of it, but all has been in a vain.

Bhagat Singh did not wish to live. He refused to apologise, or even file an appeal. Bhagat Singh was not a devotee of non-violence, but he did not subscribe to the religion of violence. He took to violence due to helplessness and to defend his homeland. In his last letter, Bhagat Singh wrote, " I have been arrested while waging a war. For me there can be no gallows. Put me into the mouth of a cannon and blow me off." These heroes had conquered the fear of death. Let us bow to them a thousand times for their heroism.

But we should not imitate their act. In our land of millions of destitute and crippled people, if we take to the practice of seeking justice through murder, there will be a terrifying situation. Our poor people will become victims of our atrocities. By making a dharma of violence, we shall be reaping the fruit of our own actions.

Hence, though we praise the courage of these brave men, we should never countenance their activities. Our dharma is to swallow our anger, abide by the discipline of non-violence and carry out our duty."

Gandhiji's role

On March 23rd Mahatma Gandhi had written a letter to the Viceroy in which he appealed for commutation for the death sentences against Bhagat Singh, Sukhdev and Rajguru. However, there have been unfounded claims that Gandhiji had an opportunity to stop Bhagat Singh's execution. In contrast, it is held that Gandhiji did not have enough influence with the British to stop the execution, much less arrange it, but that he did his best to save Bhagat Singh's life. Gandhiji supporters assert that Bhagat Singh's role in the independence movement was no threat to Gandhi's role as its leader, so he would have no reason to want him dead. Gandhiji always maintained that he was a great admirer of Singh's patriotism. He also stated that he was opposed to Bhagat Singh's execution and proclaimed that he had no power to stop it.Of Bhagat Singh's execution Gandhi said: "The government certainly had the right to hang these men. However, there are some rights which do credit to those who possess them only if they are enjoyed in name only." Gandhiji also once remarked about capital punishment: "I cannot in all conscience agree to anyone being sent to the gallows. God alone can take life, because he alone gives it."[83] Gandhi had managed to have 90,000 political prisoners, who were not members of his Satyagraha movement, released under the **Gandhi–Irwin Pact**. According to a report in the Indian magazine **Frontline**, he did plead several times for the commutation of the death sentences of Singh, Rajguru and Sukhdev, including a personal visit on 19th March 1931. In a letter to the Viceroy on the day of their execution, he pleaded fervently for commutation, not knowing that the letter would arrive too late. Lord Irwin, the Viceroy, later said:

"As I listened to Mr. Gandhi putting the case for commutation before me, I reflected first on what significance it surely was that the apostle of non-violence should so earnestly be pleading the cause of the devotees of a creed so fundamentally opposed to his own, but I should regard it as wholly wrong to allow my judgement to be influenced by purely political considerations. I could not imagine a case in which under the law, penalty had been more directly deserved."

Chapter - 18

Ideals and Opinions

Communism

Bhagat Singh regarded Kartar Singh Sarabha, the founding-member of the **Ghadar Party** as his hero. He was also inspired by **Bhai Parmanand**, another founding-member of the Ghadar Party. Bhagat Singh was attracted to anarchism and communism. He was an avid reader of the teachings of **Mikhail Bakunin** and also read **Karl Marx, Vladimir Lenin and Leon Trotsky.**

In his last testament, **"To Young Political Workers"**, he declares his ideal as the "Social reconstruction on new, i.e., Marxist, basis". Bhagat Singh did not believe in the Gandhian ideology – which advocated Satyagraha and other forms of non-violent resistance, and felt that such politics would replace one set of exploiters with another.

From May to September 1928, Bhagat Singh published a series of articles on anarchism in **Kirti**. He was concerned that the public misunderstood the concept of anarchism, writing that: "The people are scared of the word anarchism. The word anarchism has been abused so much that even in India revolutionaries have been called anarchist to make them unpopular." He clarified that anarchism refers to the absence of a ruler and abolition of the state, not the absence of order. He went on to say: "I think in India the idea of universal brotherhood, the Sanskrit sentence Vasudhaiva Kutumbakam etc., has the same meaning."

He believed that:

The ultimate goal of anarchism is complete independence, according to which no one will be obsessed with God or religion, nor will anybody be crazy for money or other worldly desires. There will be no chains on the body or control by the state. This means that they want to eliminate: the Church, God and Religion; the state; Private property.

On 21st January 1930, during the trial of the **Lahore Conspiracy Case,** Bhagat Singh and his HSRA comrades, appeared in the court wearing red scarves. When the magistrate took his chair, they raised slogans "**Long Live Socialist Revolution**", "**Long Live Communist International**", "**Long Live People**", "**Lenin's Name Will Never Die**" and "**Down with Imperialism**". Bhagat Singh then read the text of a telegram in the court and asked the magistrate to send it to the Third International. The telegram stated:

"On Lenin day we send hearty greetings to all who are doing something for carrying forward the ideas of the great Lenin. We wish success to the great experiment Russia is carrying out. We join our voice to that of the international working class movement. The proletariat will win. Capitalism will be defeated. Death to Imperialism".

Historian KN Panikkar described Singh as one of the early Marxists in India. The political theorist Jason Adams notes that he was more enamoured with Lenin than with Marx. From 1926 onward, he studied the history of the revolutionary movements in India and abroad. In his prison notebooks, he quoted Lenin in reference to imperialism and capitalism and also the revolutionary thoughts of Trotsky.

On the day of his execution, Bhagat Singh was reading the book, **Reminiscences of Lenin**, authored by Clara Zetkin, a German Marxist. When asked what his last wish was, Bhagat Singh replied that he was studying the life of Lenin and he wanted to finish it before his death.

Atheism

Bhagat Singh began to question religious ideologies after witnessing the Hindu–Muslim riots that broke out after Gandhi disbanded the Non-Cooperation Movement. He did not understand how members of these two groups, initially united in fighting against the British, could be at each other's throats because of their religious differences.[93] At this point, Singh dropped his religious beliefs, since he believed religion hindered the revolutionaries' struggle for independence, and began studying the works of **Bakunin, Lenin, Trotsky** – all atheist revolutionaries. He also took an interest in Soham Swami's book Common Sense.

While in prison in 1930–31, Bhagat Singh was approached by Randhir Singh, a fellow inmate, and a Sikh leader who would later found the **Akhand Kirtani Jatha**. According to Bhagat Singh's close associate Shiva Verma, who later compiled and edited his writings, Randhir Singh tried to convince Bhagat Singh of the existence of God, and upon failing berated him: "You are giddy with fame and have developed an ego that is standing like a black curtain between you and God". In response, Bhagat Singh wrote an essay entitled "Why I Am an Atheist" to address the question of whether his atheism was born out of vanity. In the essay, he defended his own beliefs and said that he used to be a firm believer in the Almighty, but could not bring himself to believe the myths and beliefs that others held close to their hearts. He acknowledged the fact that religion made death easier, but also said that unproven philosophy is a sign of human weakness.[95] In this context, he noted:

"As regards the origin of God, my thought is that man created God in his imagination when he realised his weaknesses, limitations and shortcomings. In this way he got the courage to face all the trying circumstances and to meet all dangers that might occur in his life and also to restrain his outbursts in prosperity and affluence. God, with his whimsical laws and parental generosity was painted with variegated colours of imagination. He was used as a deterrent factor when his fury and his laws were repeatedly propagated so that man might not become a danger to society. He was the cry of the distressed soul for he was believed to stand as father and mother, sister and brother, brother and friend when in time of distress a man was left alone and helpless. He was Almighty and could do anything. The idea of God is helpful to a man in distress."

Towards the end of the essay, Bhagat Singh wrote:

"Let us see how steadfast I am. One of my friends asked me to pray. When informed of my atheism, he said, "When your last days come, you will begin to believe." I said, "No, dear sir, Never shall it happen. I consider it to be an act of degradation and demoralisation. For such petty selfish motives, I shall never pray." Reader and friends, is it vanity? If it is, I stand for it."

"Killing the ideas"

In the leaflet he threw in the Central Assembly on 8th April 1929, he stated: "It is easy to kill individuals but you cannot kill the ideas. Great empires crumbled, while the ideas survived." While in prison, Singh and two others had written a letter to Lord Irwin, wherein they asked to be treated as prisoners of war and consequently to be executed by firing squad and not by hanging. Prannath Mehta, Singh's friend, visited him in the jail on 20th March, three days before his execution, with a draft letter for clemency, but he declined to sign it.

Chapter - 19

Popularity

Subhas Chandra Bose said that: "Bhagat Singh had become the symbol of the new awakening among the youths." Nehru acknowledged that Bhagat Singh's popularity was leading to a new national awakening, saying: "He was a clean fighter who faced his enemy in the open field ... he was like a spark that became a flame in a short time and spread from one end of the country to the other dispelling the prevailing darkness everywhere". Four years after Singh's hanging, the Director of the Intelligence Bureau, Sir Horace Williamson, wrote: "His photograph was on sale in every city and township and for a time rivaled in popularity even that of Mr. Gandhi himself."

Chapter - 20

Modern Days

The youth of India still draw tremendous amount of inspiration from Bhagat Singh. He was voted the "Greatest Indian" in a poll by the Indian magazine India Today in 2008, ahead of Bose and Gandhi. During the centenary of his birth, a group of intellectuals set up an institution named **Bhagat Singh Sansthan** to commemorate him and his ideals. The Parliament of India paid tributes and observed silence as a mark of respect in memory of Singh on 23rd March 2001 and 2005. In Pakistan, after a long-standing demand by activists from the Bhagat Singh Memorial Foundation of Pakistan, the Shadman Chowk square in Lahore, where he was hanged, was renamed as Bhagat Singh Chowk. This change was successfully challenged in a Pakistani court.[119][120] On 6th September 2015, the Bhagat Singh Memorial Foundation filed a petition in the Lahore high court and again demanded the renaming of the Chowk to Bhagat Singh Chowk.

Films and Television

Several films have been made portraying the life and times of Singh. The first film based on his life was **Shaheed-e-Azad Bhagat Singh (1954)** in which Prem Adeeb played the role of Singh followed by **Shaheed Bhagat Singh (1963)**, starring Shammi Kapoor as Bhagat Singh, **Shaheed (1965)** in which Manoj Kumar portrayed Bhagat Singh and Amar **Shaheed Bhagat Singh (1974)** in which Som Dutt portrays Singh. Three films about Singh were released in 2002 **Shaheed-E-Azam, 23 March 1931: Shaheed** and **The Legend of Bhagat Singh** in which Singh was portrayed by Sonu Sood, Bobby Deol and Ajay Devgn respectively. **Bhagat Singh (2002)**, a drama film directed by Anand Sagar and written/produced Ramanand Sagar was aired on DD National. It featured Deepak Dutta in the titular role.

Siddharth played the role of Bhagat Singh in the 2006 film **Rang De Basanti,** a film drawing parallels between revolutionaries of Bhagat

Singh's era and modern Indian youth. Another similar approach was taken in the independent film, among others, **Shaheed-E-Aazam (2018)** where Rahul Pathak played the lead role. Gurdas Mann played the role of Singh in **Shaheed Udham Singh**, a film based on life of Udham Singh while Amol Parashar portrayed Singh in Sardar Udham, another film based on Udham Singh's life. Karam Rajpal portrayed Bhagat Singh in Star Bharat's television series **Chandrashekhar**, which is based on life of ChandraShekhar Azad.

In 2008, **Nehru Memorial Museum and Library (NMML)** and **Act Now for Harmony and Democracy (ANHAD)**, a non-profit organisation, co-produced a 40-minute documentary on Bhagat Singh entitled Inqilab, directed by Gauhar Raza.

Theatre

Bhagat Singh, Sukhdev and Rajguru have been the inspiration for a number of plays in India and Pakistan, that continue to attract crowds.

Songs

Although not written by Singh, the patriotic Hindustani songs, **"Sarfaroshi Ki Tamanna"** ("The desire to sacrifice") created by Bismil Azimabadi,[133] and **"Mera Rang De Basanti Chola"** ("O Mother! Dye my robe the colour of spring") created by Ram Prasad Bismil,[134] are largely associated with him and have been used in a number of related films.

Others

In 1968, a **postage stamp** was issued in India commemorating the 61st birth anniversary of Bhagat Singh. A ₹5 coin commemorating him was released for circulation in 2012.